Madala
Adult Coloring

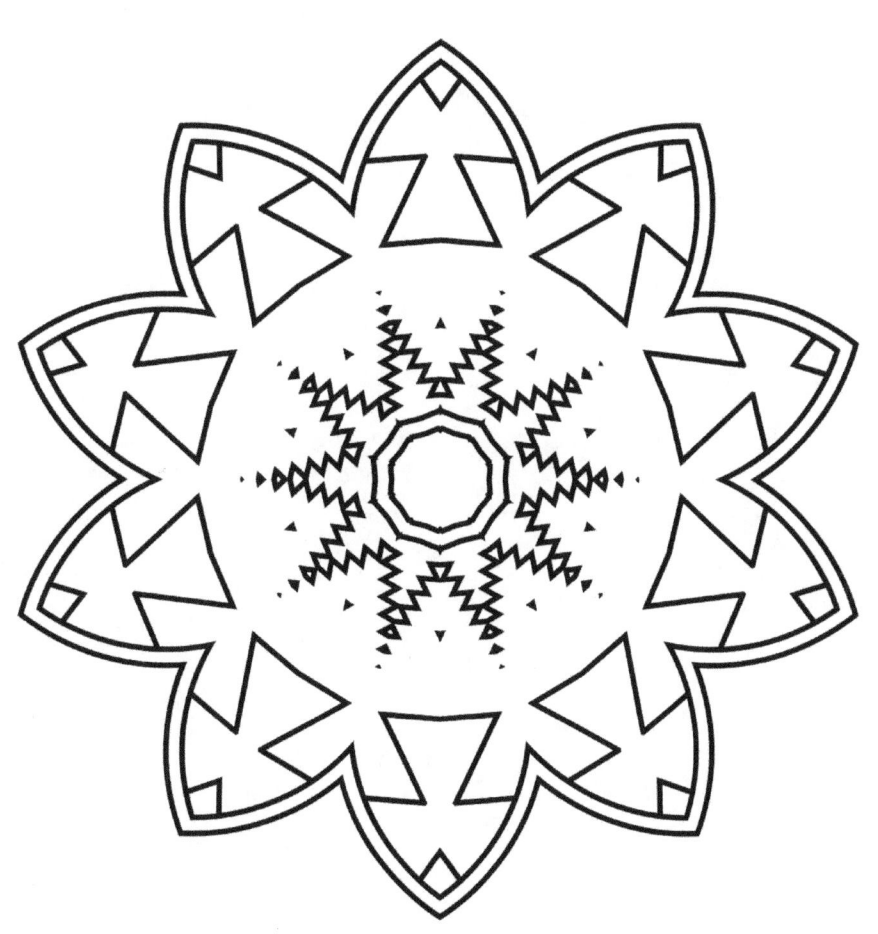

Belinda L. Frazier

Madala
Adult Coloring

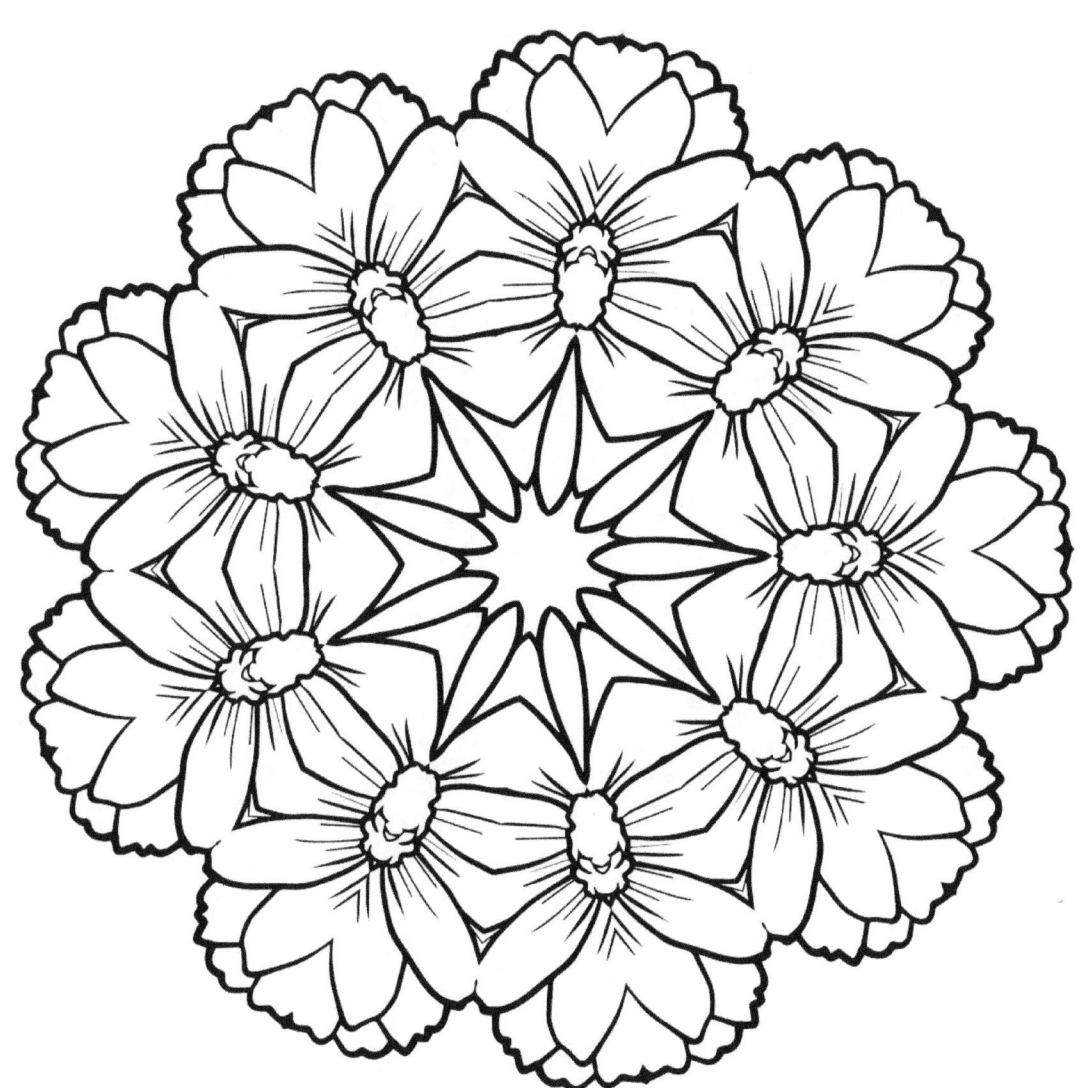

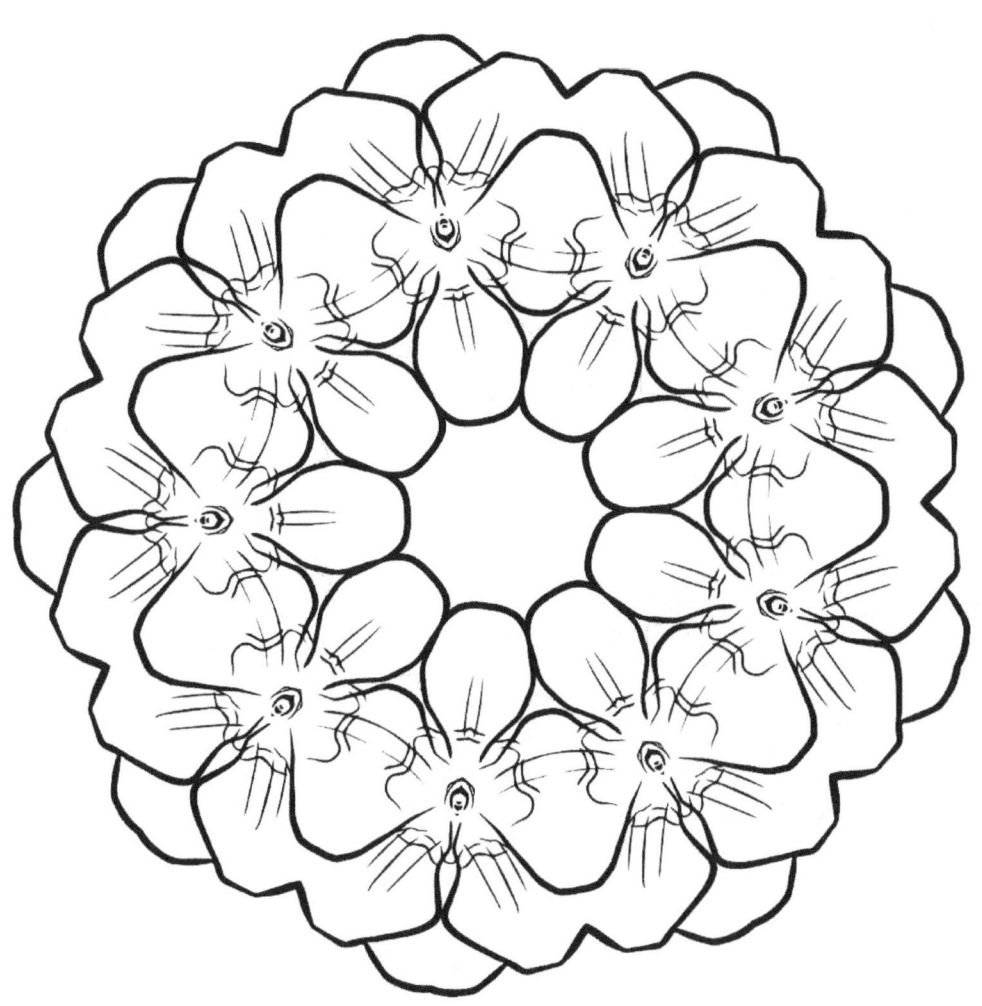

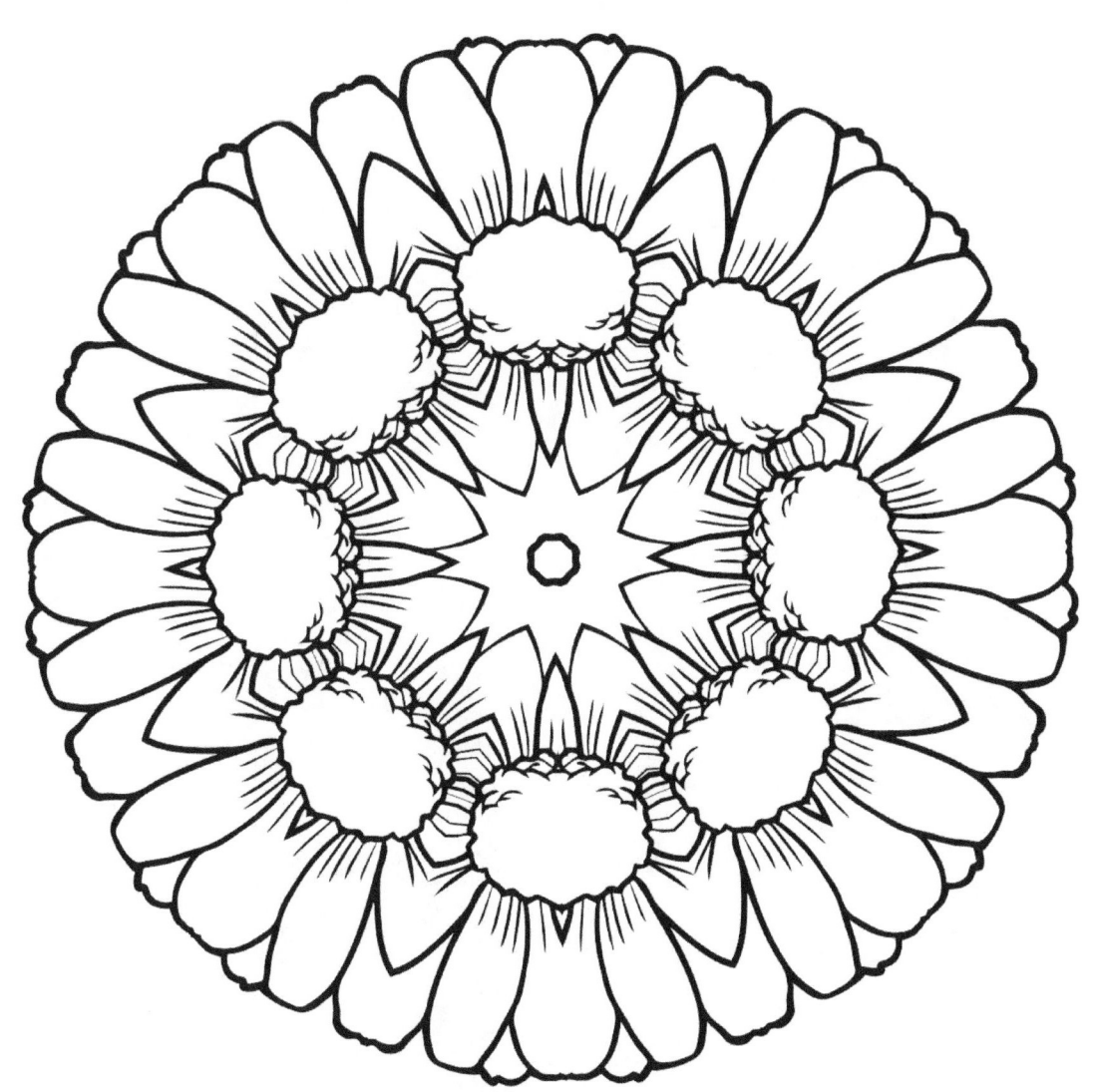

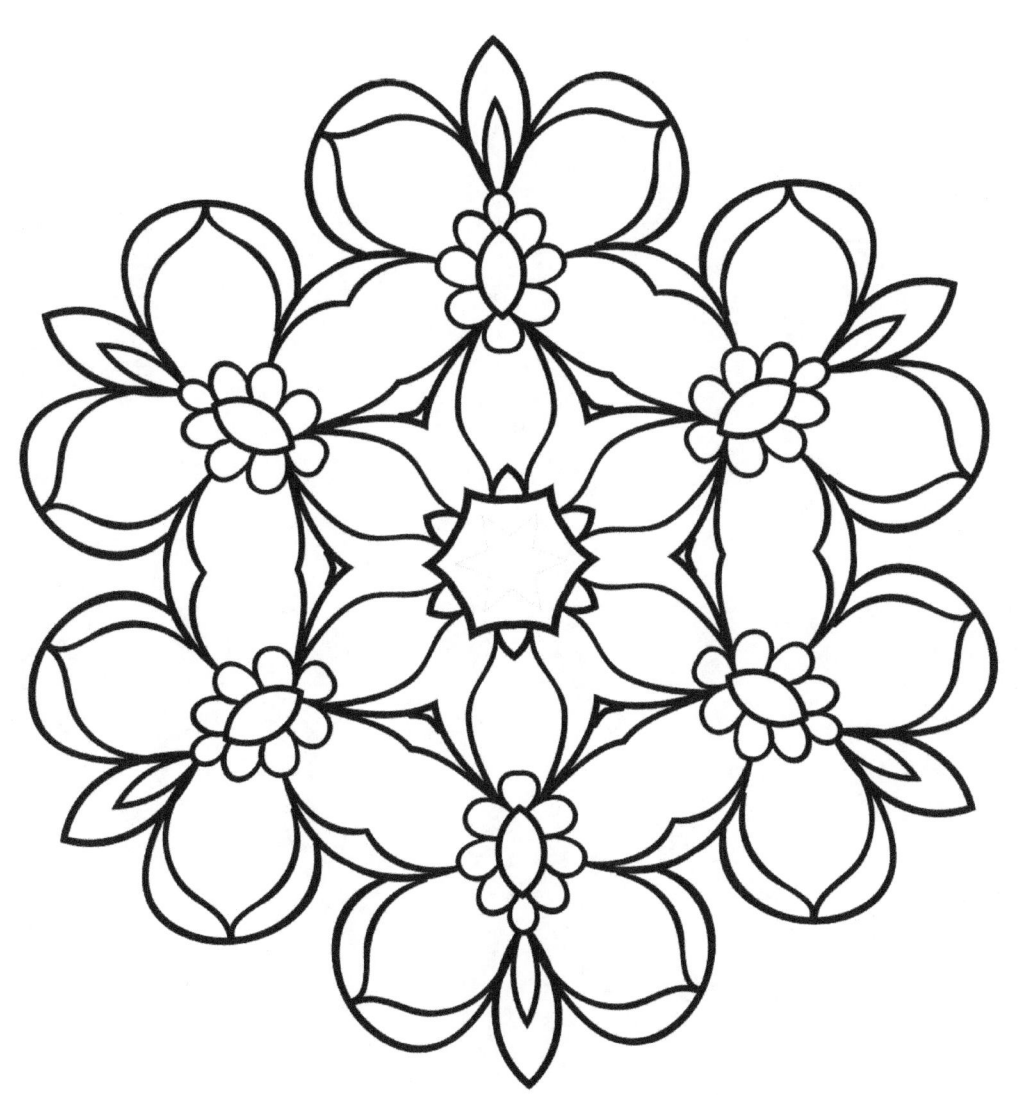

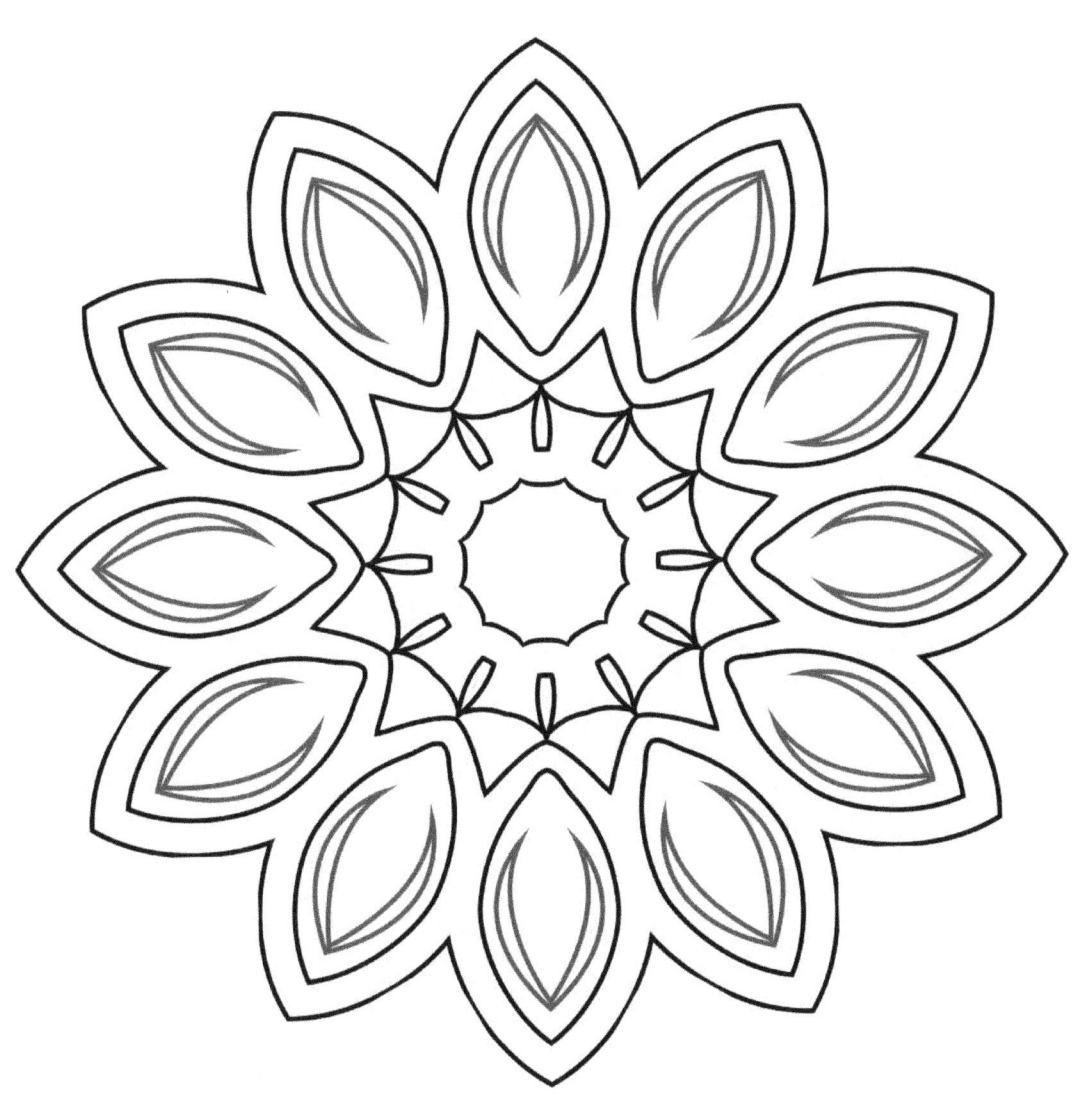

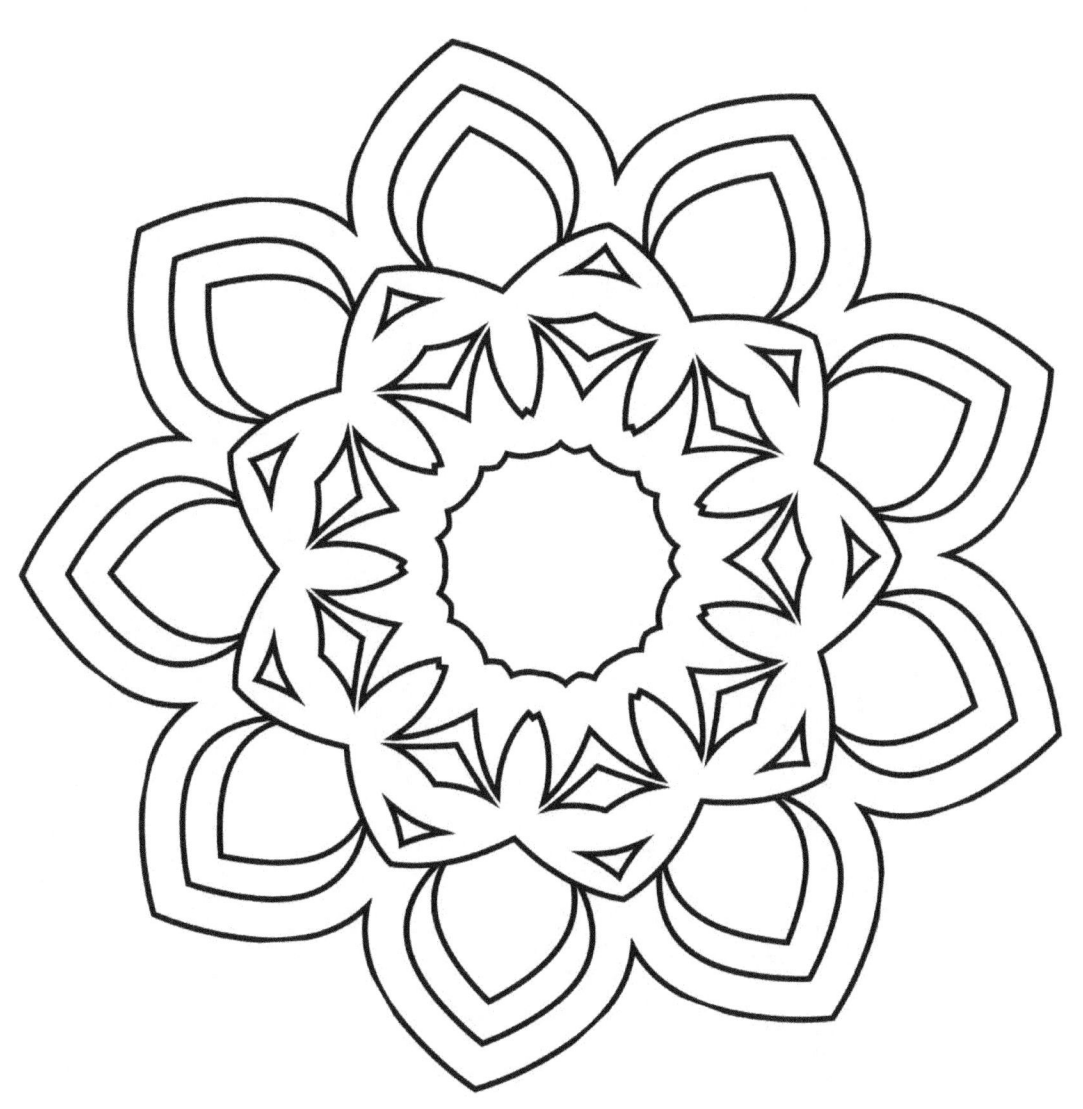

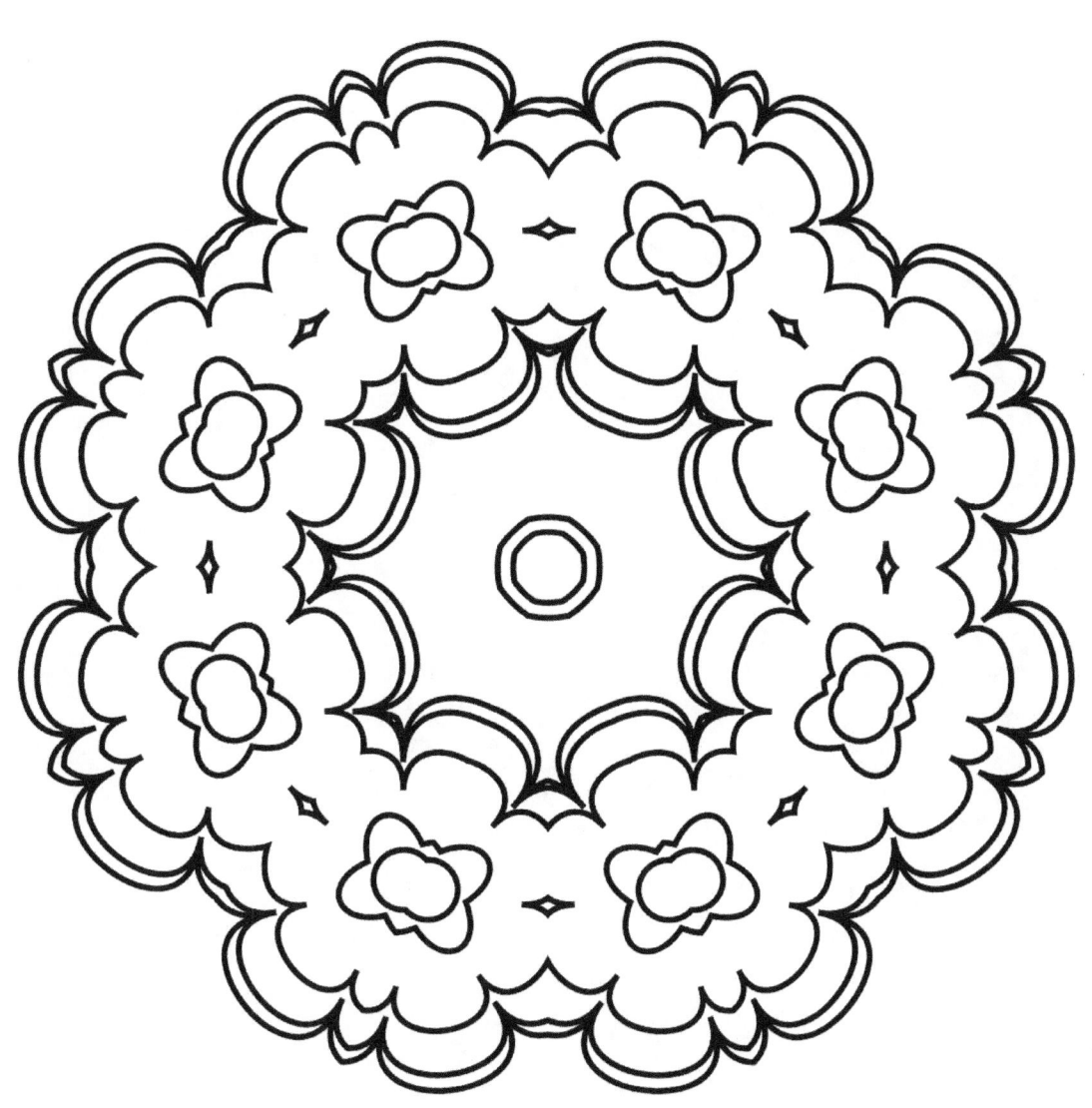

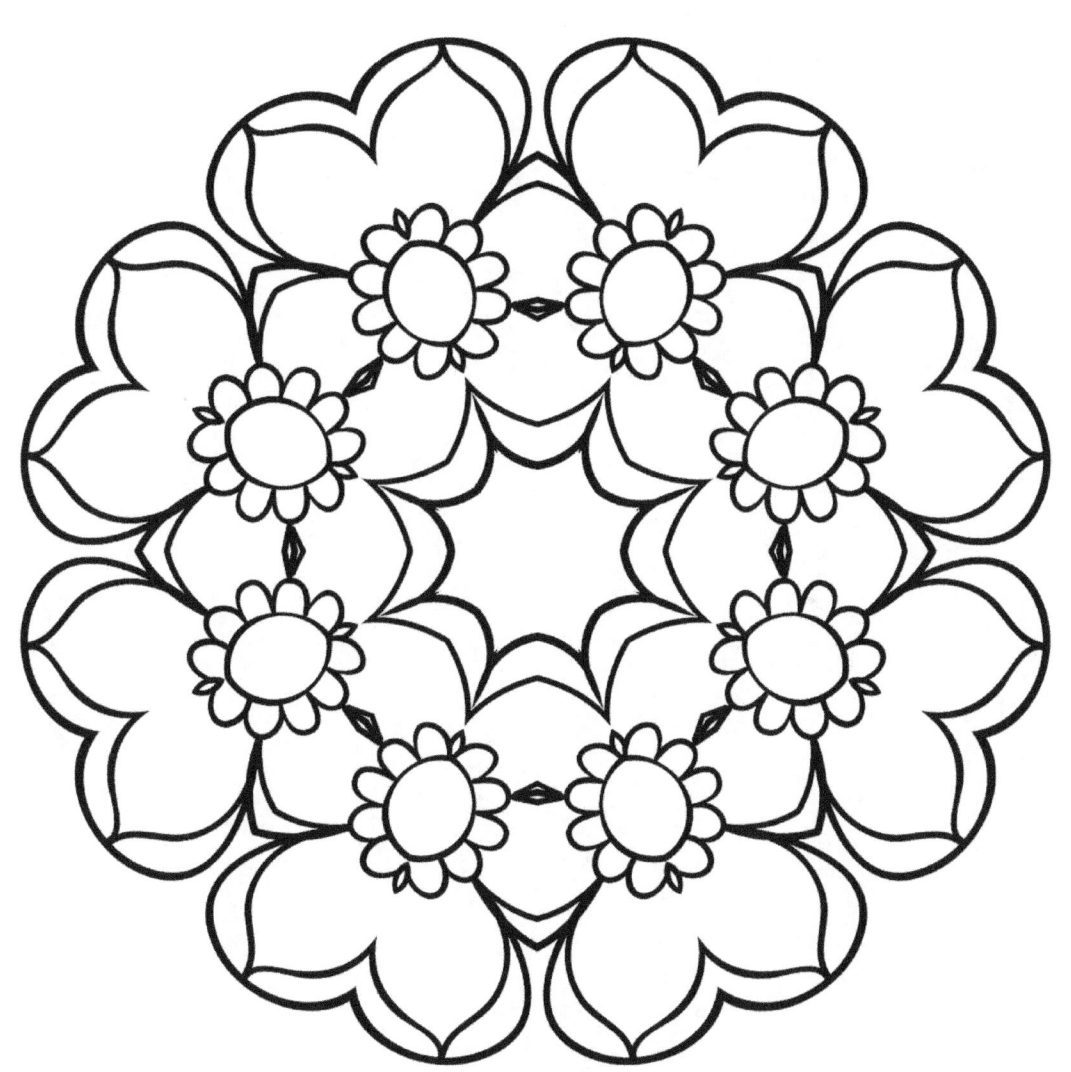

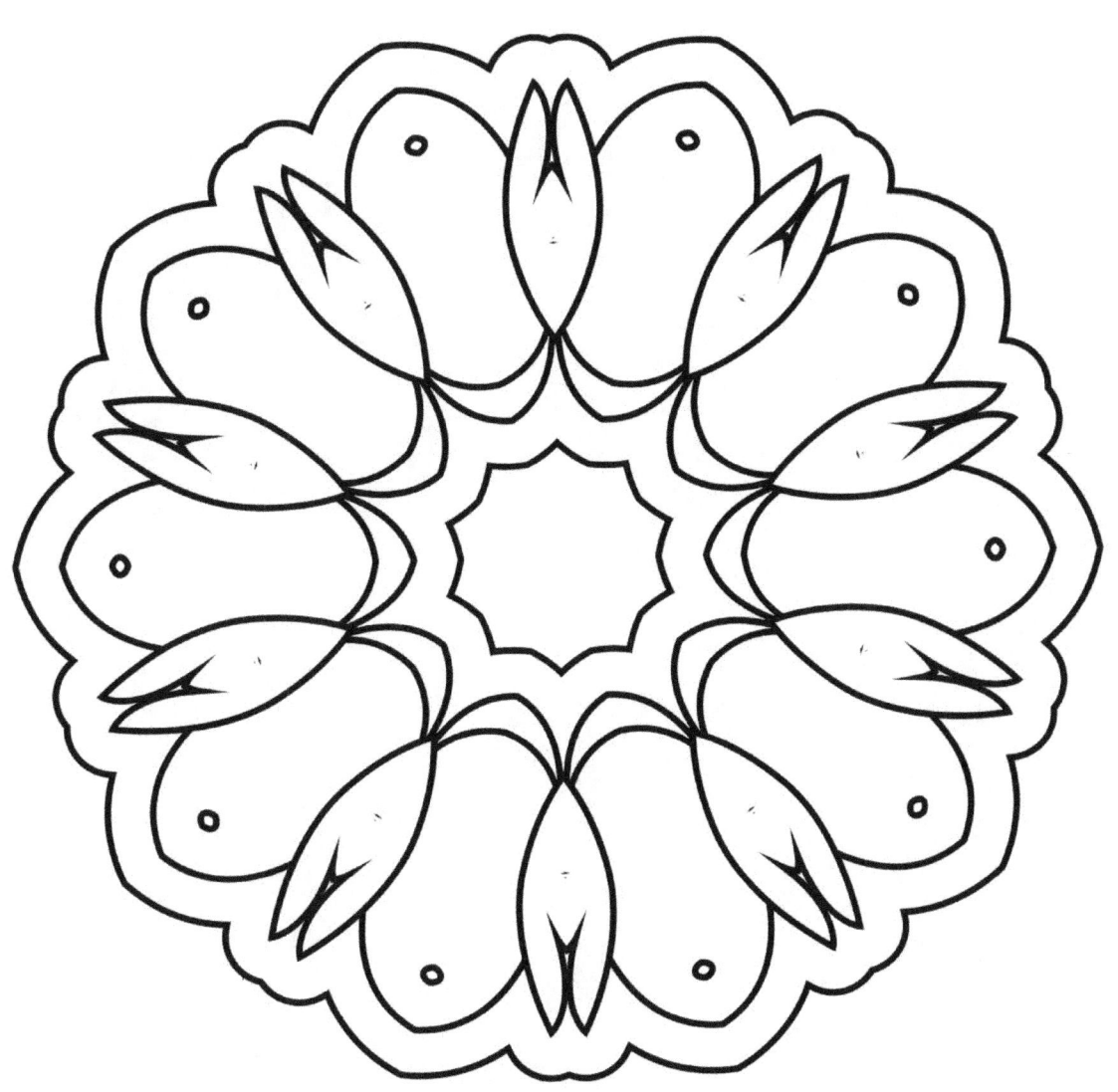

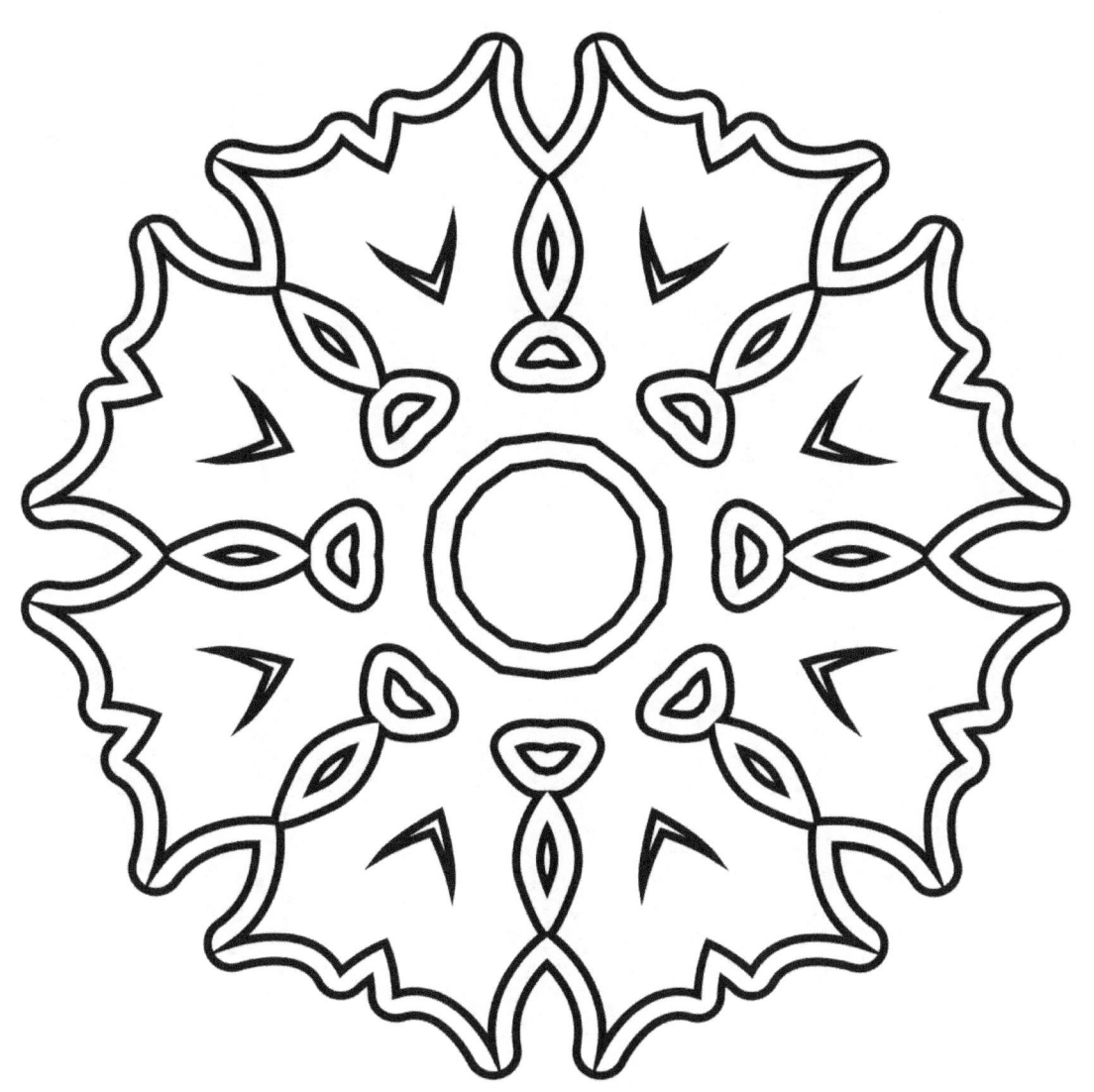

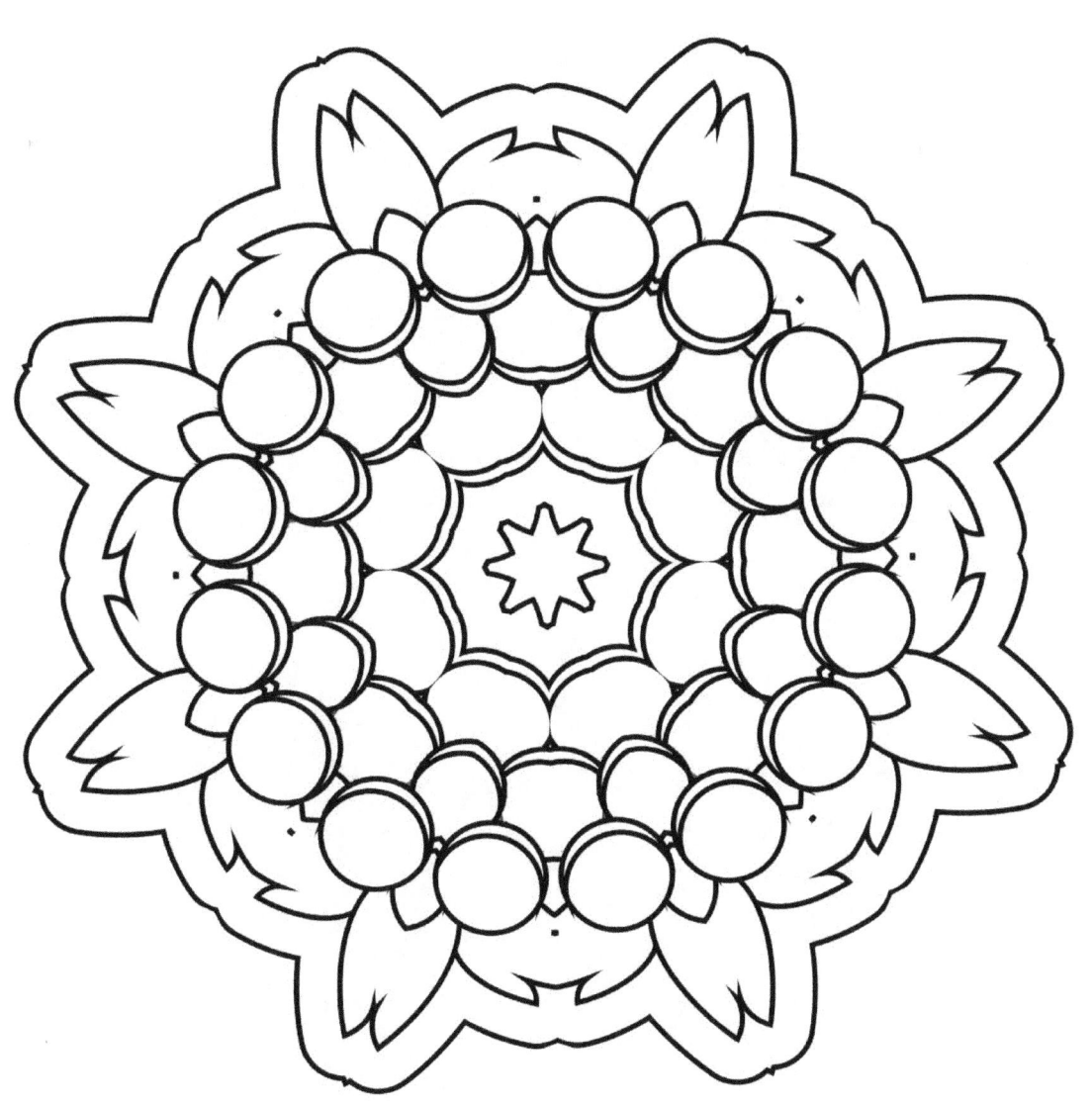

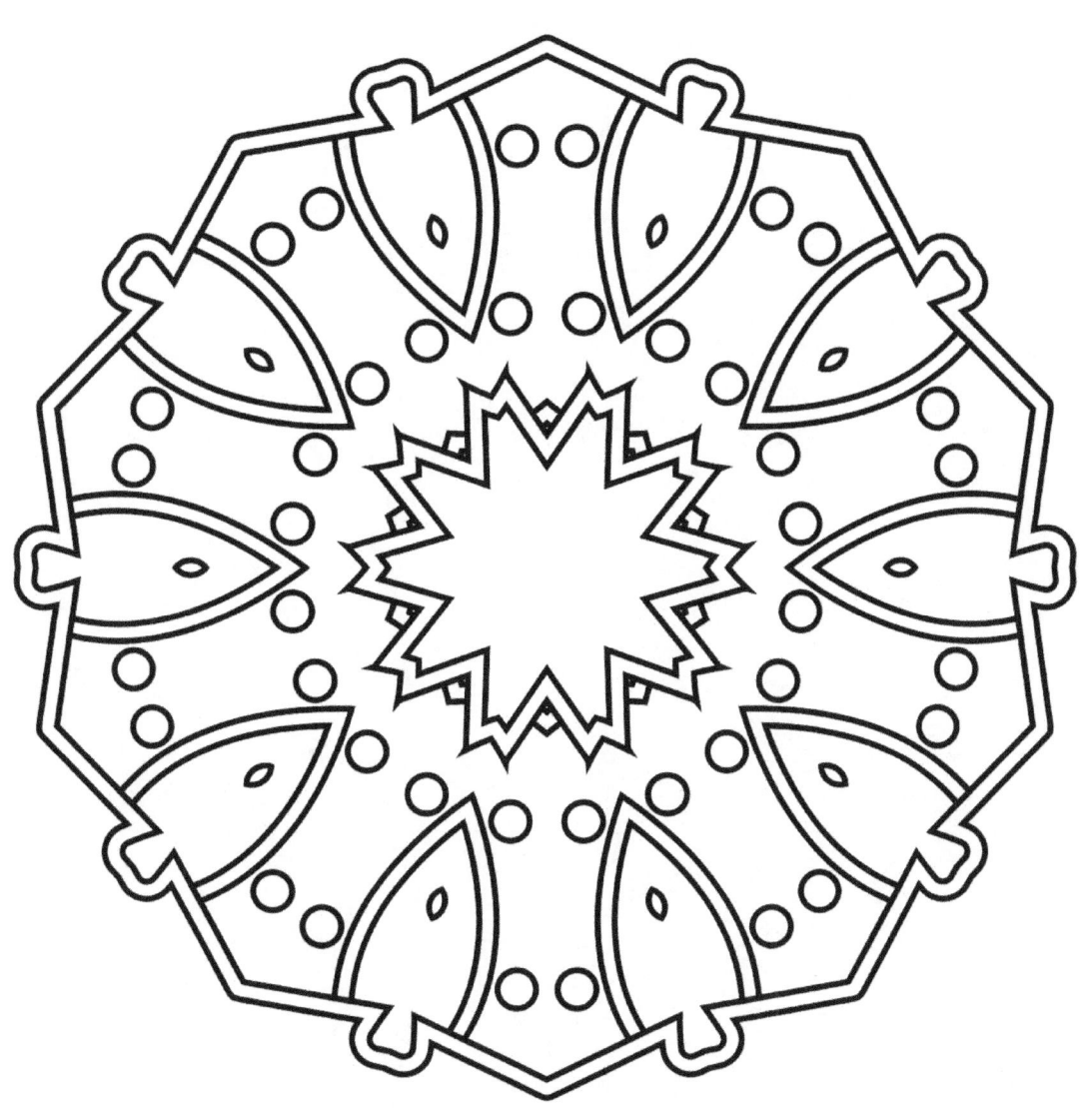

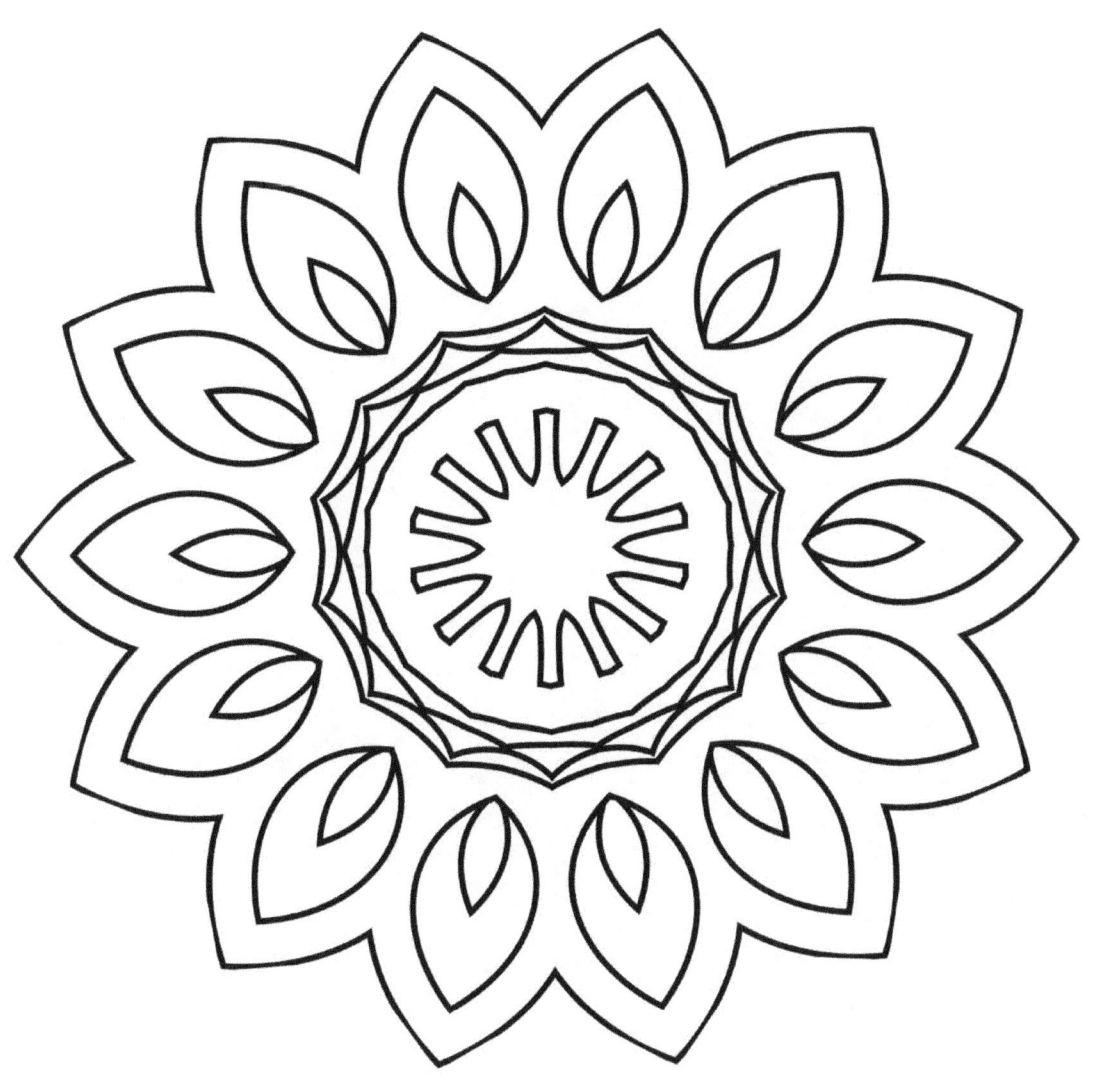

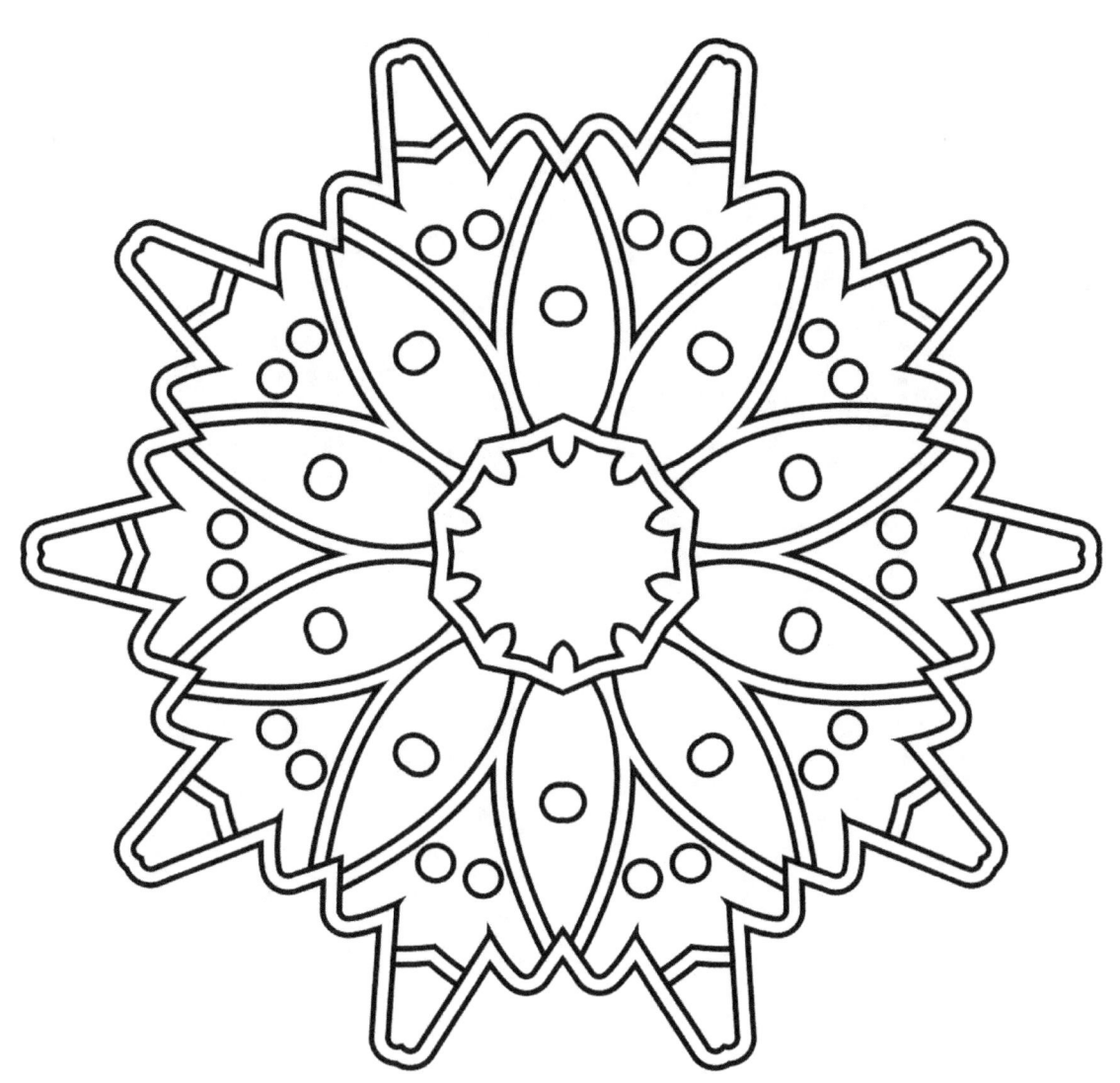

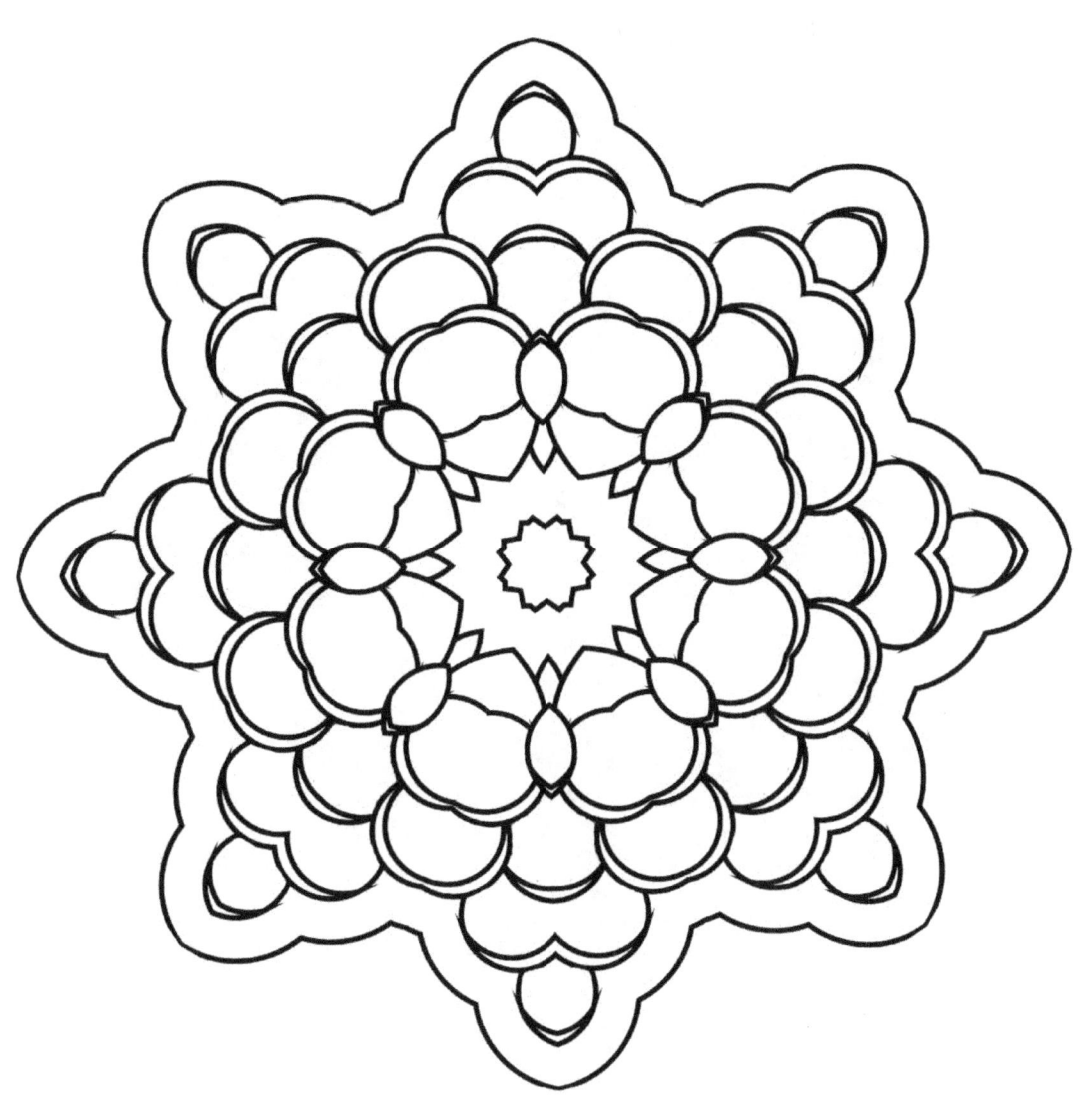

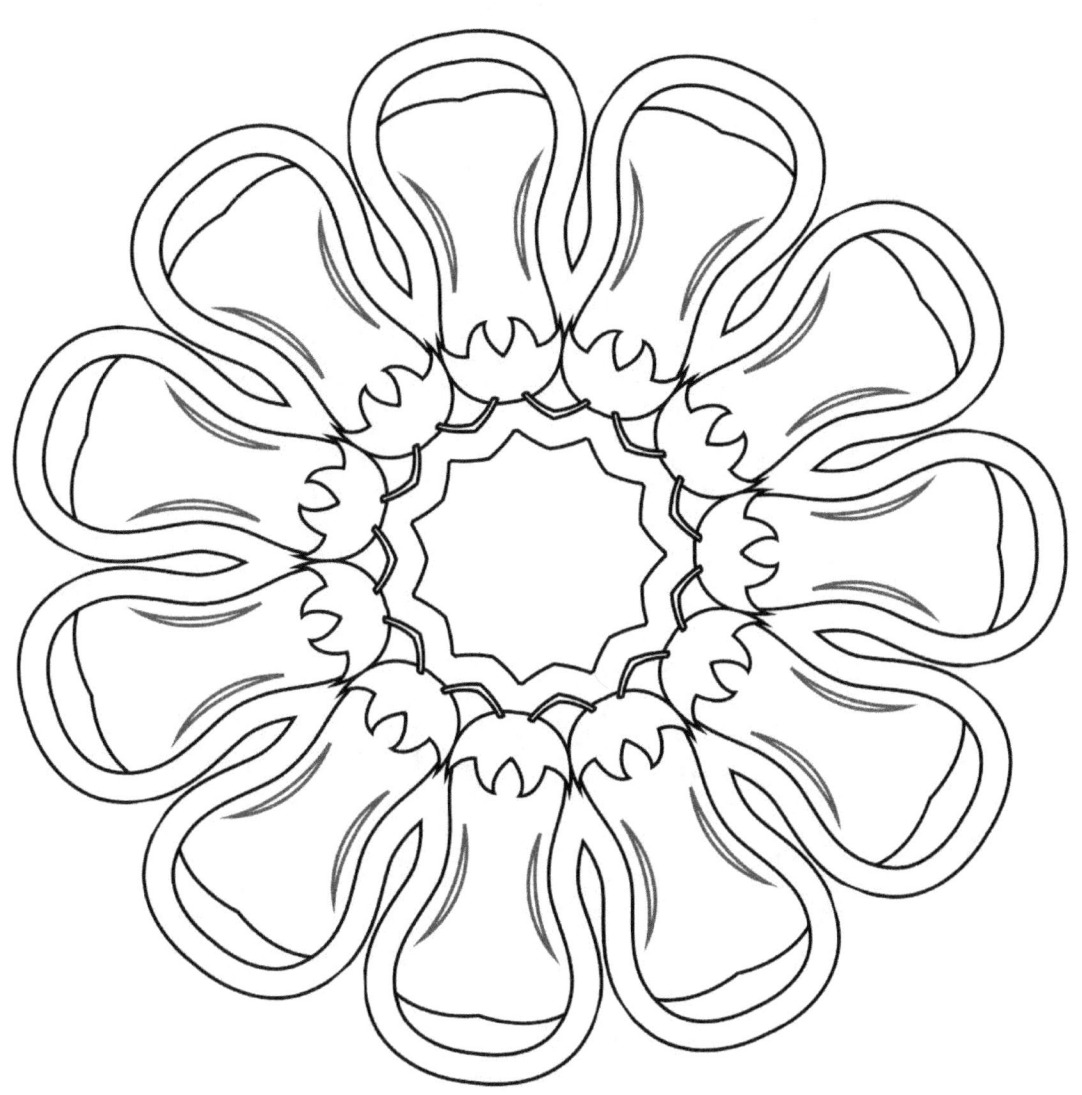

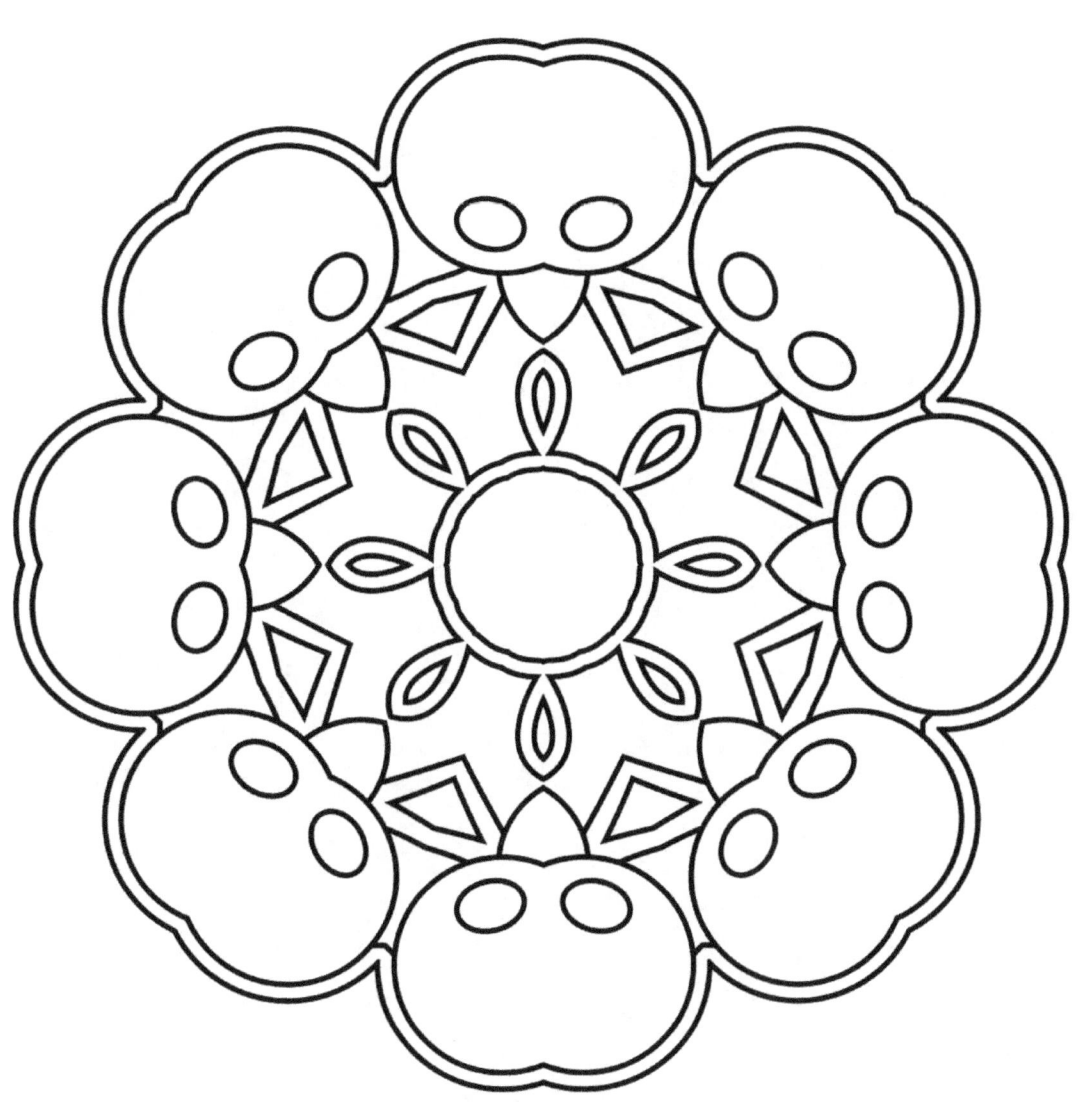

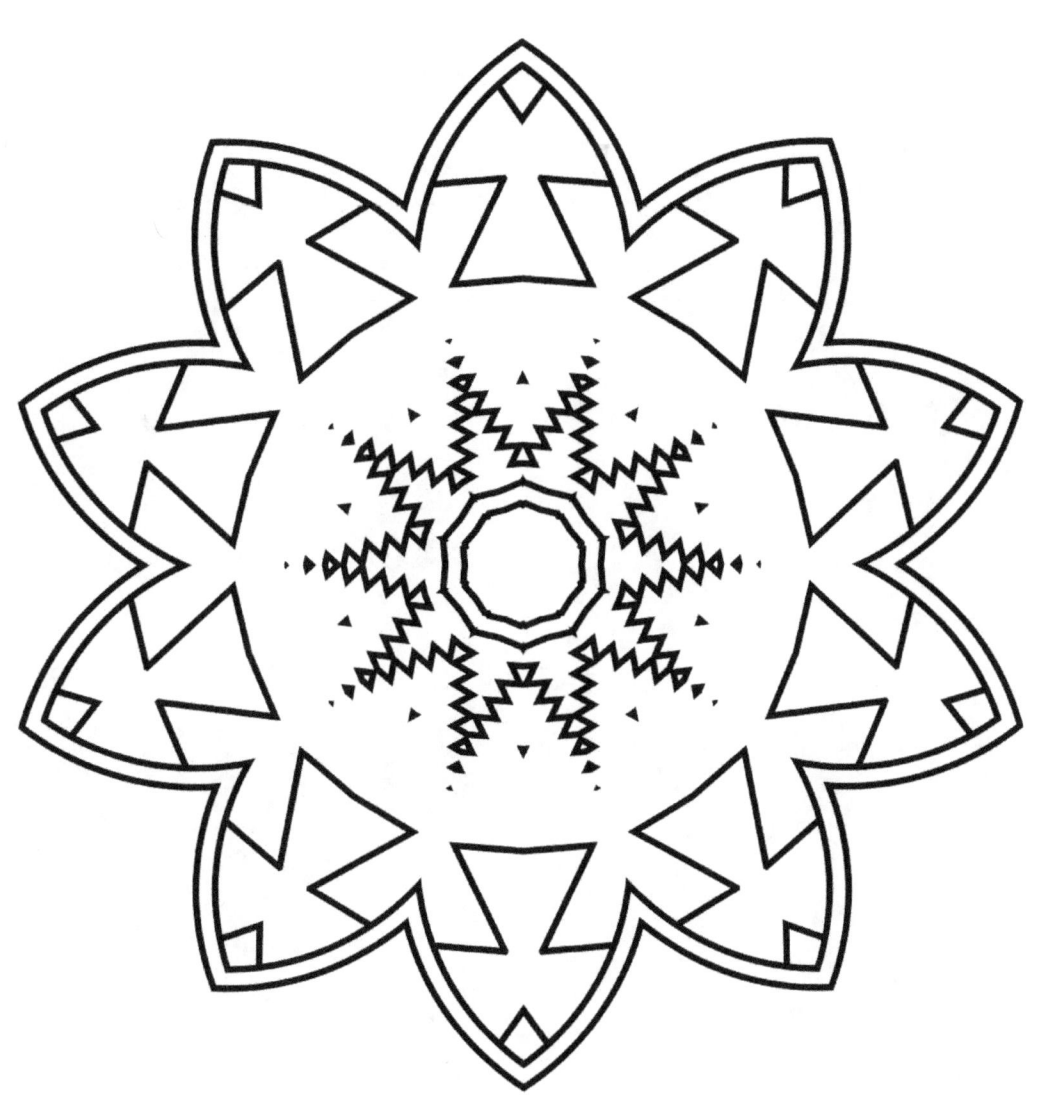

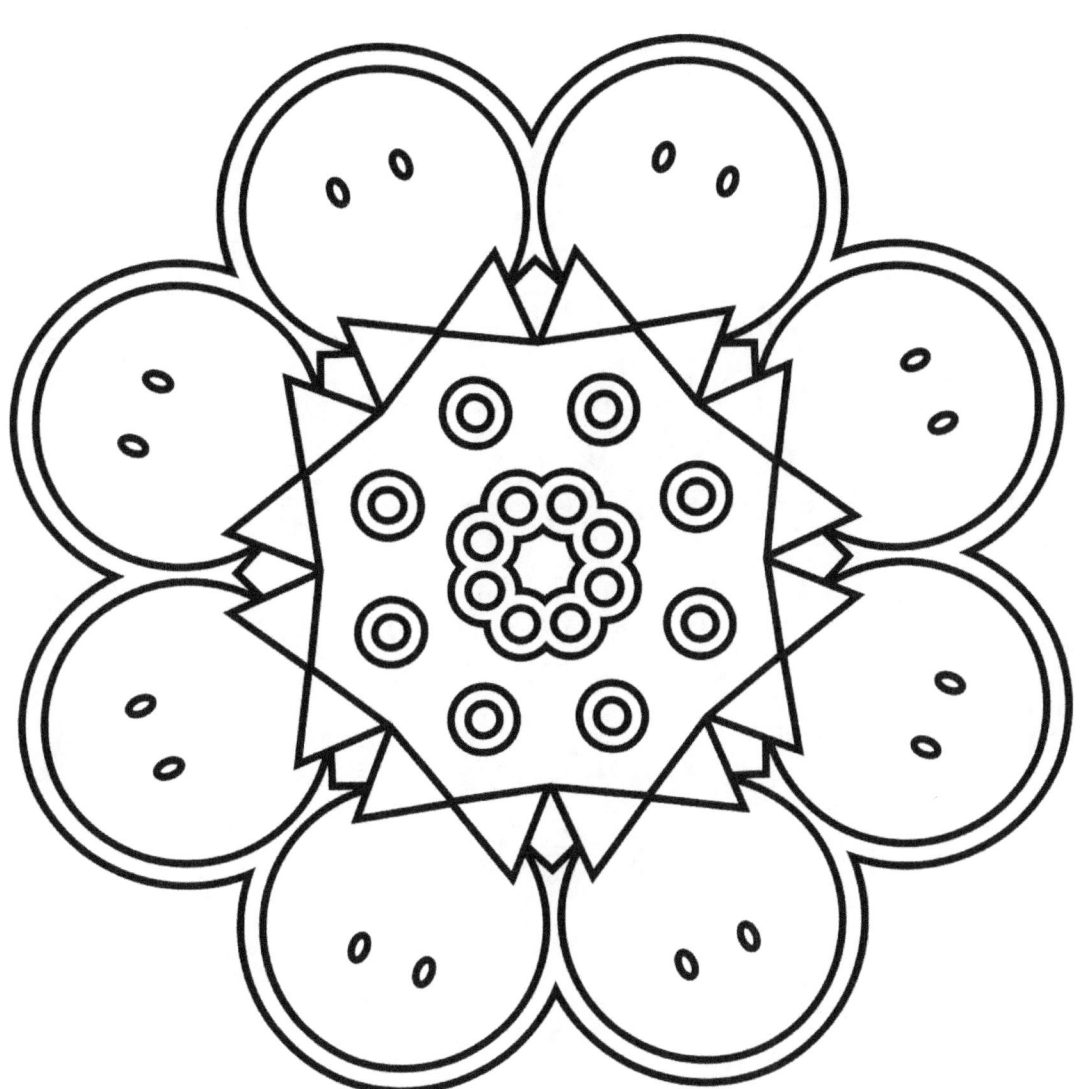

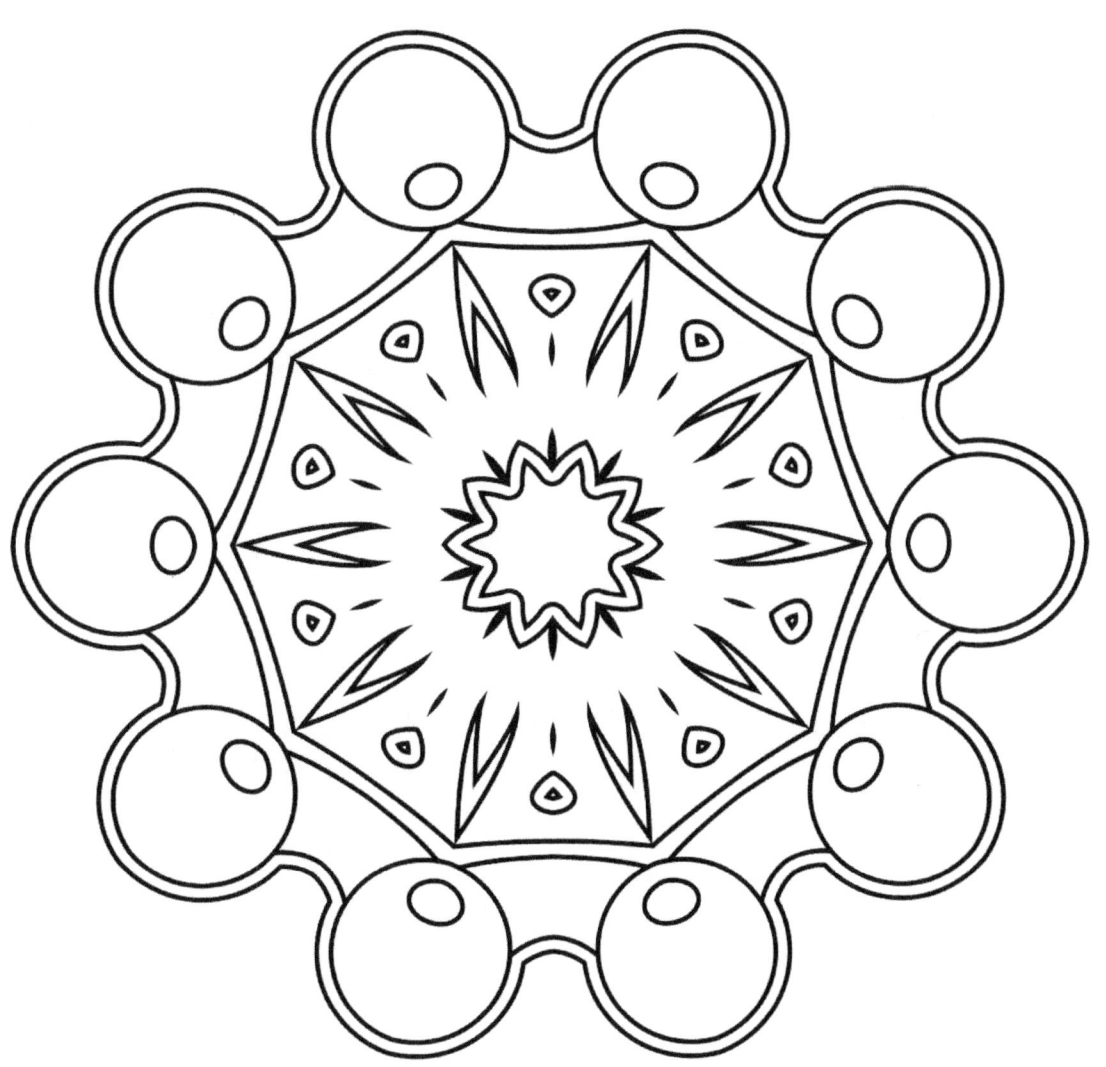

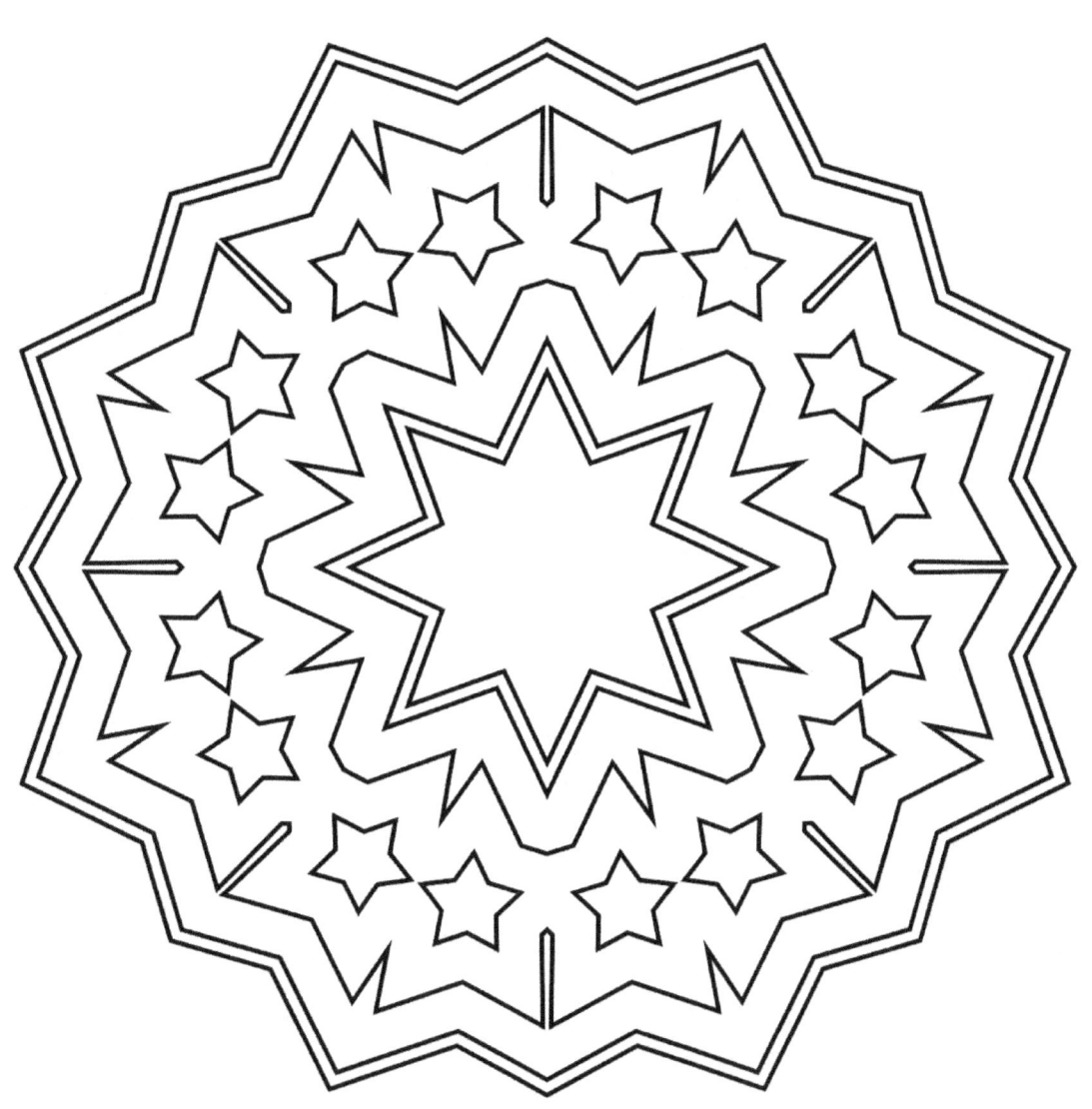

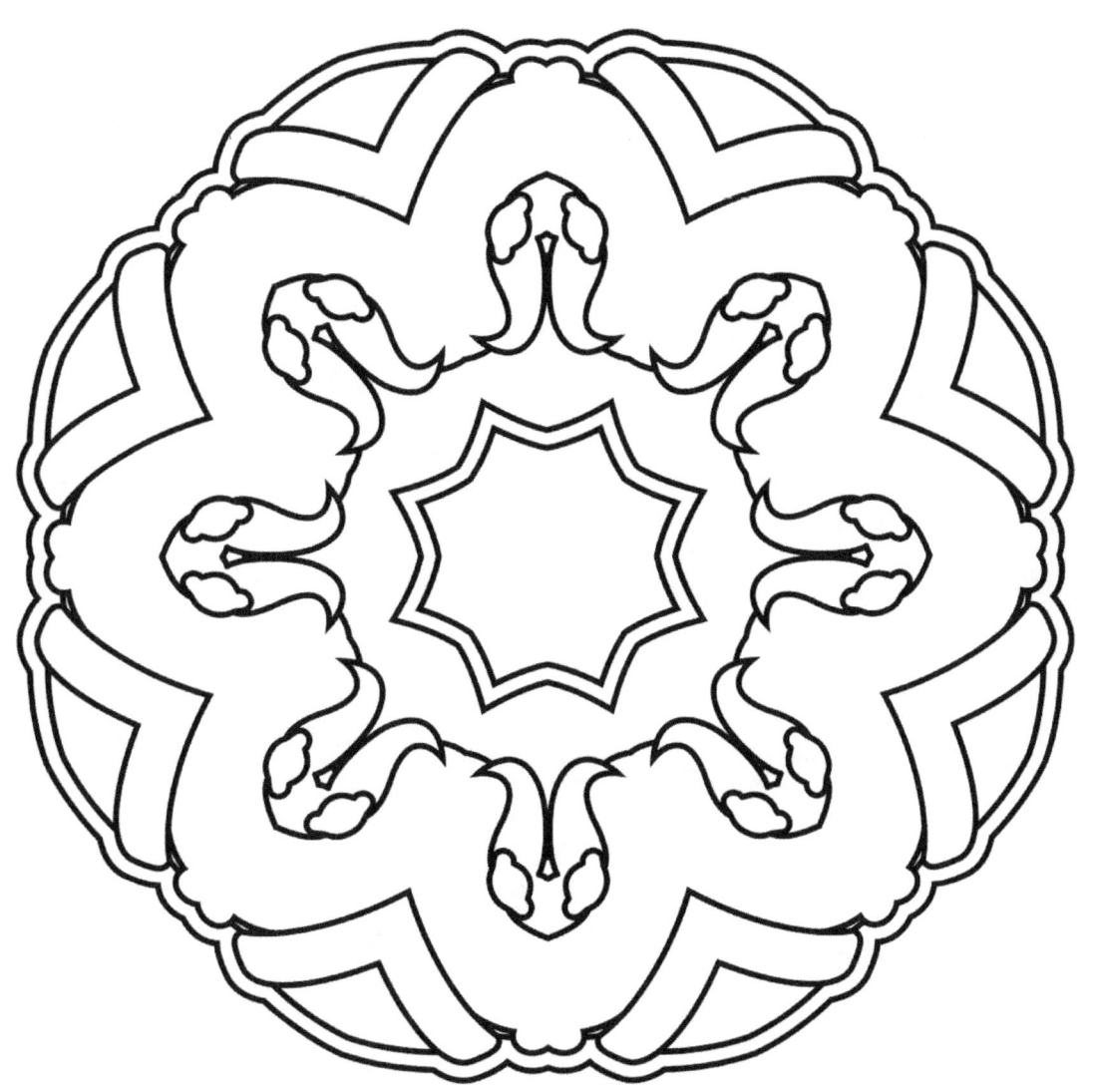

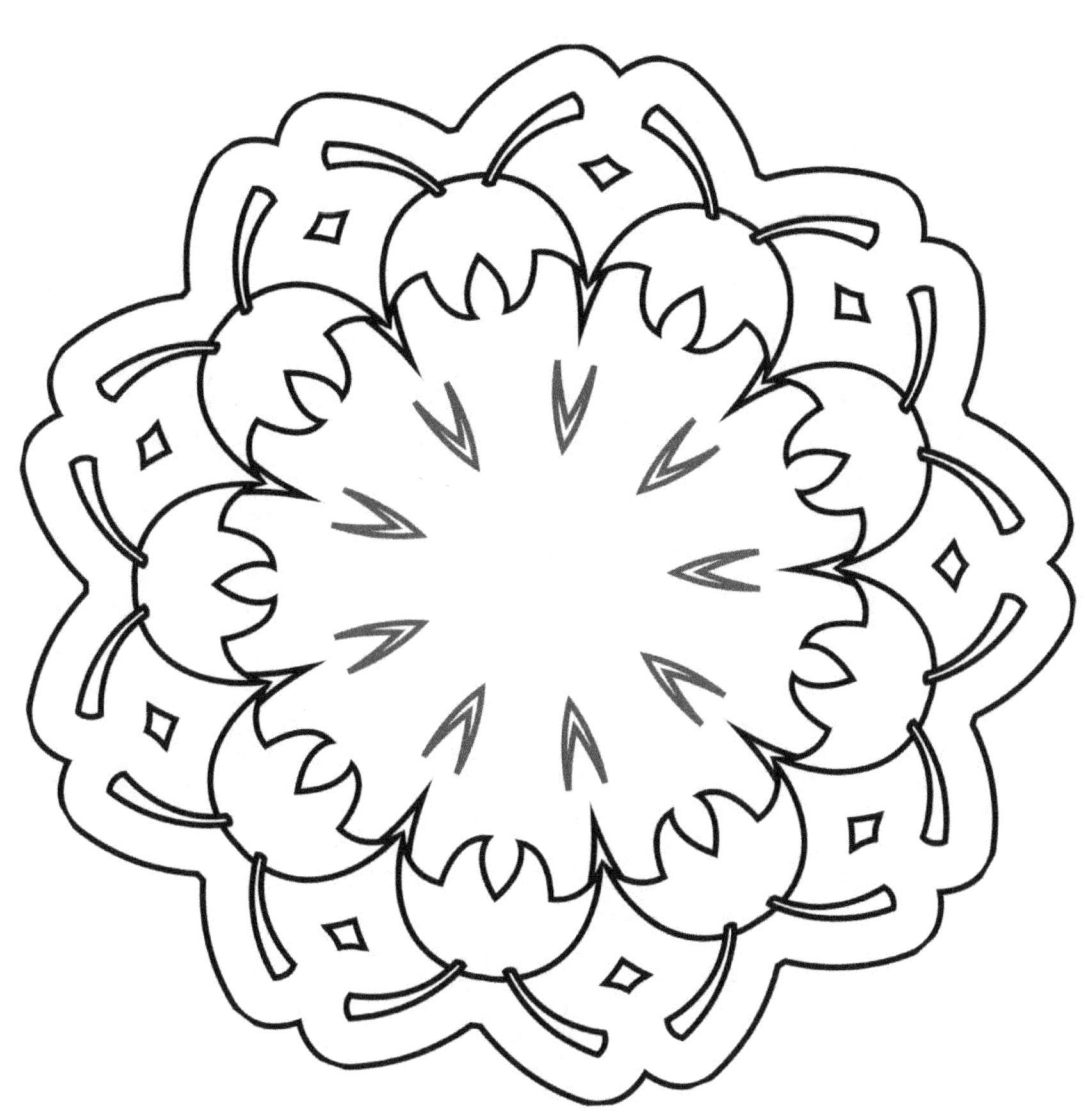

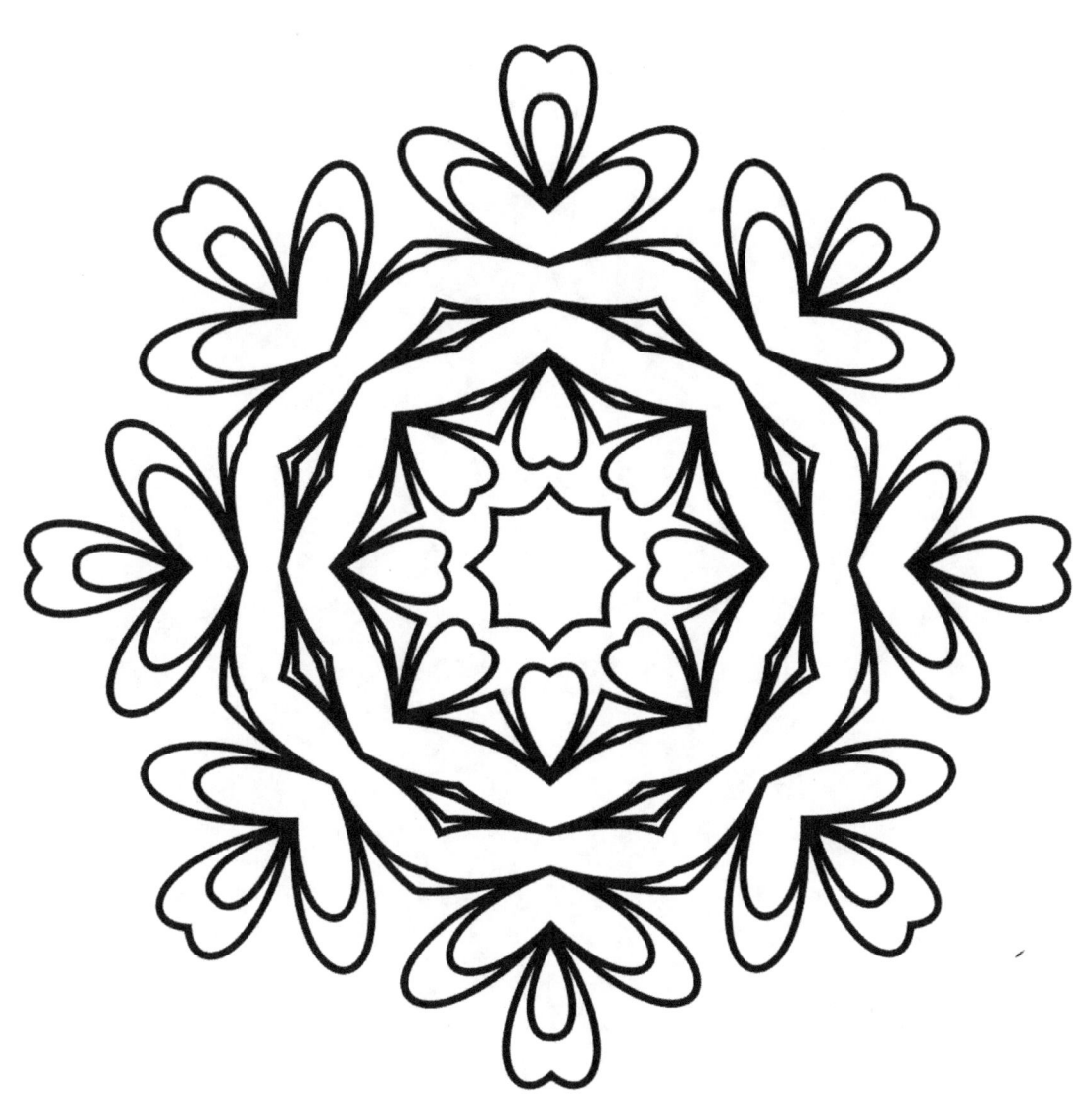

A Note About The Author

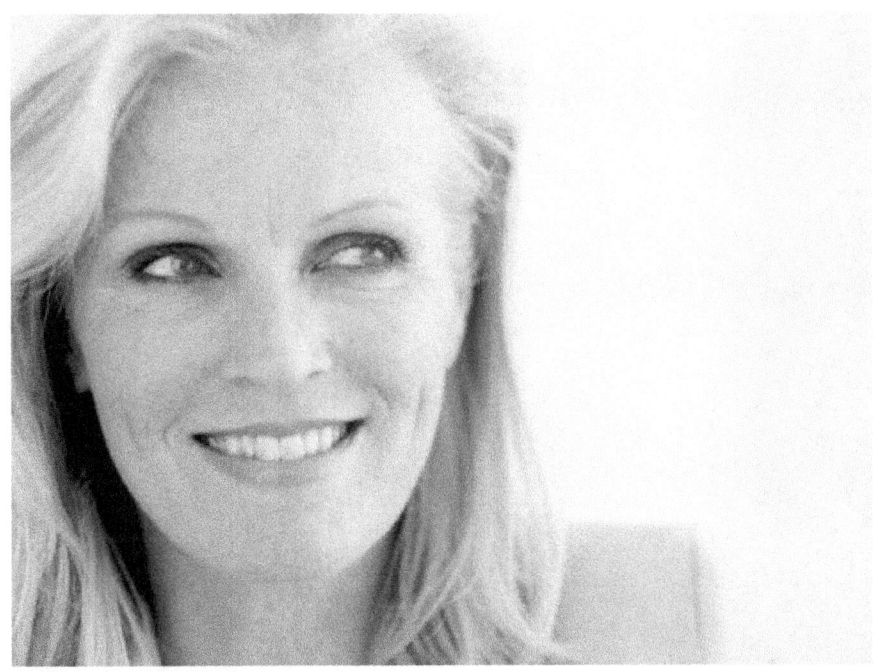

Belinda L. Frazier
Feel free to contact Belinda L. Frazier at belinda.coloring@gmail.com

Check out their Amazon profile here:

http://www.amazon.com/-/e/B01FSO94TA